W9-CKI-334

NUMBER CRUNCH YOUR WAY AROUND

AUSTRALIA

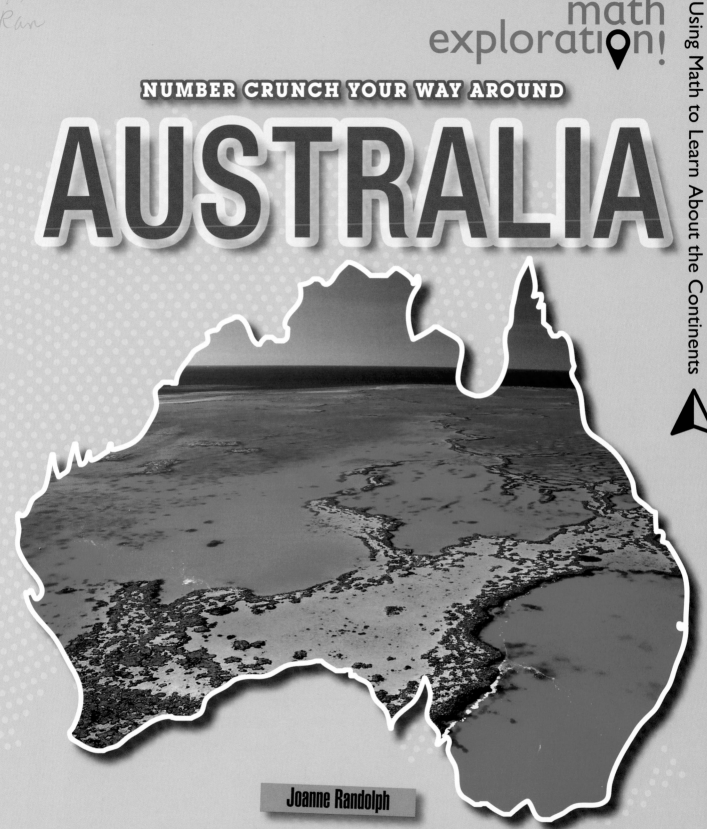

Joanne Randolph

PowerKiDS
press

New York

Published in 2016 by **The Rosen Publishing Group**
29 East 21st Street, New York, NY 10010

Produced for Rosen by Calcium

Editors for Calcium: Sarah Eason, Rosie Hankin, and Katie Dicker
Designer: Paul Myerscough

Art by Moloko88/Shutterstock

Photo credits: Cover: Shutterstock: Anan Kaewkhammul (top), Stanislav Fosenbauer (back cover), Selfiy
(bottom); Inside: Dreamstime: Mogens Trolle 26l; Shutterstock: Richard J Ashcroft 14br, Attem 16c,
Anton Balazh 7b, Baronb 16t, Ingvars Birznieks 15t, David Bostock 9b, Edmund Chai 23b, Curioso 17b,
Dangdumrong 19tr, Larissa Dening 17c, EcoPrint 22c, Edella 15b, Susan Flashman 24l, Stanislav Fosenbauer
4c, 28-29c, GeorgeMPhotography 8t, Gevision 18t, 28-29b, Edward Haylan 5c, 29c, Ben Heys 21t, JC Photo
1, 11c, Anan Kaewkhammul 28l, Kwest 23t, Johan Larson 18b, Steve Lovegrove 25c, Robyn Mackenzie 19b,
Christopher Meder 26r, Marcella Miriello 20c, N Mrtgh 12c, Masaki Norton 7t, Regien Paassen 27b, Pics
by Nick 14bl, Production Perig 21b, Jordi Prat Puig 27t, Jason Patrick Ross 21c, Selfiy 4b, Vlad61 10c, Ashley
Whitworth 5t, Ian Woolcock 24b, Worldswildlifewonders 6c, Peter Zaharov 13c, Jun Zhang 6b, Zstock 9t,
23c; Wikimedia Commons: David Iliff 13br.

Cataloging-in-Publication Data
Randolph, Joanne.
Number crunch your way around Australia / by Joanne Randolph.
p. cm. — (Math exploration: using math to learn about the continents)
Includes index.
ISBN 978-1-4994-1243-7 (pbk.)
ISBN 978-1-4994-0705-1 (6 pack)
ISBN 978-1-4994-1262-8 (library binding)
1. Australia — Juvenile literature. 2. Mathematics — Juvenile literature.
I. Randolph, Joanne. II. Title.
DU96.R36 2016
994—d23

Manufactured in the United States of America
CPSIA Compliance Information: Batch WS15PK: For Further Information contact Rosen Publishing, New York, New York at 1-800-237-9932

Contents

Australia

Welcome to Australia! This amazing **continent** is also an island, surrounded by the Pacific Ocean and the Indian Ocean. Are you ready to use your map and math skills to explore the **geography** of Australia? Your math exploration challenge starts now!

Indian Ocean

How to Use This Book

Look for the "Map-a-Stat" and "Do the Math" features and complete the math challenges. Then look at the answers on pages 28 and 29 to see if your calculations are correct.

Uluru

Lush and Dry

The spectacular Great Barrier Reef is found on Australia's northeast coast. Also on the east coast is the beautiful city of Sydney, where the stunning Sydney Opera House is found. Australia's north has some lush rain forests, filled with many **exotic** birds and plants. The interior of Australia is mainly dry and flat, with much of it covered in a desert-like landscape called the outback, or the bush. There, the amazing, world-famous rock formation Uluru, or Ayers Rock, is found. Many animals live in the outback, too, including snakes, **dingoes**, and wombats.

Sydney Opera House

rain forest

Map-a-Stat

Australia has a total land area of almost 3 million square miles (7.6 million sq km).

For every 132 square miles (342 sq km) of land, there are just 1,000 people.

The Sydney Opera House is 219 feet (67 m) high, 606 feet (185 m) long, and 394 feet (120 m) wide.

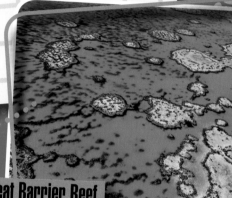

Pacific Ocean   the Great Barrier Reef

Australia

DO THE MATH!

Use the information in red in the Map-a-Stat box to figure out the following challenge. If the Sydney Opera House had a rectangular base, could you calculate its perimeter? Here is the equation to help you solve the problem.

$$606 \text{ feet} + 606 \text{ feet} + 394 \text{ feet} + 394 \text{ feet} = ? \text{ feet}$$

Complete the math challenge, then turn to pages 28—29 to see if your calculation is correct!

World's Smallest Continent

Australia is the sixth-largest country in the world, but it is the smallest continent. It is a little smaller than the main body of the United States, and 32 times larger than the United Kingdom.

Home Sweet Home

Aside from the mainland, there are thousands of islands in the oceans near Australia. Scientists call this region Oceania. Australia and its island **territories** have many different **habitats**, from deserts to rain forests. These habitats are home to thousands of plant and animal **species**, many of which are found nowhere else on Earth!

Koalas often come to mind when people think of Australia. These animals eat eucalyptus leaves.

Dingoes are one of the biggest predators in Australia. They live in deserts and grasslands.

Map-a-Stat

At its widest points, Australia is almost the same length from north to south as it is from east to west. From north to south, it measures 2,398 miles (3,859 km), and from east to west it measures 2,485 miles (3,999 km).

As part of Australia, Fraser Island is the world's largest sand island. It has an area of 710 square miles (1,840 sq km).

Australia's mainland is divided into 5 states and 3 territories. Tasmania makes a sixth state. Plus, there are 6 island territories and the Australian Antarctic Territory.

Australia is home to many kinds of **reptiles**, with 917 species.

Fraser Island is off the east coast of Australia.

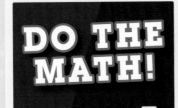

DO THE MATH!

Use the information in red in the Map-a-Stat box to figure out the following challenge. How many Australian states and territories are there altogether? Here is the equation to help you.

$$5 + 3 + 1 + 6 + 1 = ? \text{ states and territories}$$

Complete the math challenge, then turn to pages 28–29 to see if your calculation is correct!

Tasmania

The Coast with the Most

Twelve Apostles, Victoria

As an island, Australia has a lot of coasts. Ocean water often brings a more **temperate climate**. This means that it is not as hot on the coast of Australia as it is farther inland. It gets more rain, too. Because of this difference in climate, most Australians make their homes along the coast. If you look at the map of Australia below, you will notice that all the big cities and towns are found around the edges.

Australia's Cities

The capital city in Australia is Canberra. It is a two-hour drive from the ocean, but it is still part of the coastal region. New South Wales, of which Sydney is the capital, is the region where Europeans first settled on the continent. Melbourne is the second-largest city, and the capital of Victoria. Rainy, warm Brisbane is the capital of Queensland. Perth, the capital of Western Australia, lies on the Swan River, and is a busy city. Adelaide is known for its churches.

Darwin

Brisbane

Perth

Adelaide

Sydney

Canberra

Melbourne

Map-a-Stat

The mainland of Australia has a coastline that stretches 22,826 miles (36,735 km).

All of Australia's many islands make up a total of 14,825 miles (23,858 km) of coastline.

Kimberley is a region in Australia along the northwest coast. An area of the coast has a nickname, "the 80-mile (129 km) beach." Kimberley's coastline is 137 miles (220 km) long, and is home to a large number of shorebirds.

Brisbane, Australia's third-largest city, has a population of 2.13 million.

DO THE MATH!

Use the information in red in the Map-a-Stat box to figure out the following challenge. How many hours would it take you to walk the coastline of Australia's mainland if you walked at a rate of 2 miles per hour? Here is the equation to help you solve the problem.

$$22{,}826 \text{ miles} \div 2 \text{ miles per hour} = \text{? hours}$$

Complete the math challenge, then turn to pages 28–29 to see if your calculation is correct!

The Great Barrier Reef

Great Barrier Reef

Australia

The world's biggest **coral reef**, the Great Barrier Reef, is found off the coast of Australia. This extraordinary structure stretches more than 1,250 miles (2,011 km) along the northeastern Australian coast.

Full of Life

The reef is home to many animals. It has more than 600 kinds of coral, 100 kinds of jellyfish, 3,000 varieties of shellfish, 500 species of worms, 133 varieties of sharks and rays, and more than 30 species of whales and dolphins. At least 6 species of sea turtles come to the reef to breed as well.

An incredible 215 species of birds, including 22 species of seabirds and 32 species of shorebirds, visit the reef or nest on its islands. The reef also houses at least 27,300 species of fish. That is 6 percent of the world's total fish species!

Jellyfish and tropical fish are just some of the animals that live on the Great Barrier Reef.

Map-a-Stat

The Great Barrier Reef is made up of more than 2,900 individual reefs.

The Great Barrier Reef is at least 1,250 miles (2,011 km) long.

The Great Barrier Reef has more than 900 islands.

The Great Barrier Reef is around ½ the size of Texas.

The Great Barrier Reef is so large that it can even be seen from space!

DO THE MATH!

Use the information in red in the Map-a-Stat box to figure out the following challenge. If you were to swim along the Great Barrier Reef at a rate of 1 mile per hour, and back again to your starting point, how many hours would it take you to complete your journey? Here is the equation to help you solve the problem.

(1,250 miles x 1 mile per hour) x 2 = ? hours

Complete the math challenge, then turn to pages 28–29 to see if your calculation is correct!

Mountains and Highlands

Australia is the flattest and lowest continent in the world. Its average **elevation** is just 1,083 feet (330 m) above sea level. That said, Australia is known for its beautiful, rocky outcroppings, such as Uluru. It also has a few highlands and mountains worth noting. Mt. Kosciuszko is the tallest mountain on Australia's mainland and is more than 7,310 feet (2,228 km) tall.

Stirling Range National Park, Western Australia, is a bird sanctuary for species such as the short-billed black cockatoo and the western whipbird.

Uluru

Great Dividing Range

Stirling Range

Blue Mountains

Grampians

Mt. Kosciuszko

The Great Dividing Range

The Great Dividing Range, or Great Divide, is made up of **plateaus** and low mountains that run from Cape York Peninsula in Queensland to the Grampians, a mountain range in Victoria. The Great Dividing Range is 2,300 miles (3,700 km) long. Many of Australia's rivers start in the range.

Map-a-Stat

Mt. Kosciuszko is 7,310 feet (2,228 m) tall. Compare this to Mt. Everest, the tallest mountain in the world, which stands 29,035 feet (8,850 m) tall.

Mt. Townsend is Australia's second-tallest mountain at 7,266 feet (2,214 m).

Uluru rises 1,142 feet (348 m) above the surrounding **plains** and measures 5.8 miles (9.4 km) around its base.

the Snowy River, near Mt. Kosciuszko

DO THE MATH!

Use the information in red in the Map-a-Stat box to figure out the following challenge. How many times taller is Mt. Everest than Mt. Kosciuszko? You will need to round your answer. Here is the equation to help you solve the problem.

29,035 feet ÷ 7,310 feet = ? times taller

Complete the math challenge, then turn to pages 28—29 to see if your calculation is correct!

Three Sisters, Blue Mountains

Outback

Australia is the second-driest continent in the world, after Antarctica, where little rain falls. This means it is the driest continent that people live on. Around 80 percent of the continent receives less than 2.3 inches (6 cm) of rain each year. Much of Australia has few people and roads. This dry wilderness area is called the outback.

Deserts

There are 10 deserts in Australia. Few people live in these areas, though **aboriginal** groups make their homes there. They have found ingenious ways to survive in the desert, including setting fire to the bush to encourage new plants, and therefore food, to grow. Despite the tough conditions in the Australian desert, plenty of plants and animals make their home there, too.

kangaroo

The Devils Marbles, or Karlu Karlu, were shaped by natural forces.

Map-a-Stat

Only 3 percent of Australia's population lives in the desert. These people include aborigines.

Around 460,000 aborigines live in Australia. There are about 500 different groups of aborigines.

More **mammals** have become **extinct** in Australia in the last 400 years than any other continent in the world. In fact, ⅓ of all the world's extinct mammals were Australian.

According to the International Union for Conservation of Nature (IUCN) Red List, Australia has 10 mammal, 4 bird, 13 fish, 7 reptile, and 15 **amphibian** species that are critically endangered, or almost extinct.

Sturt's Desert Pea is one of Australia's best known wildflowers.

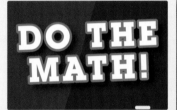

DO THE MATH!

Use the information in red in the Map-a-Stat box to figure out the following challenge. Add up the different species that are critically endangered in Australia. Here is the equation to help you solve the problem.

$$10 + 4 + 13 + 7 + 15$$
$$= ? \text{ species}$$

Complete the math challenge, then turn to pages 28—29 to see if your calculation is correct!

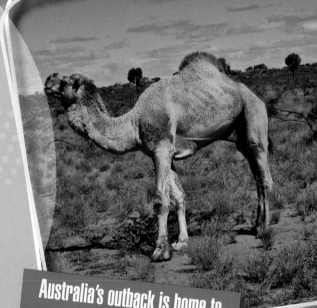

Australia's outback is home to a colony of wild camels.

Farmland

Despite the country's dry conditions, agriculture is an important industry in Australia. Australian farmers grow crops. They also raise cattle for milk and meat, and sheep for milk, meat, and wool. Australia's land is most **fertile** along the coasts and in Tasmania. The grasslands of the interior lowlands are used for grazing. With **irrigation**, less fertile land can still be farmed though it is challenging.

sheep

grasslands in Western Australia

Farms and Food

Much of Australia's coastal areas can get up to 12.5 inches (32 cm) of rain each year. This allows many kinds of crops to be grown and provides rich pasture for dairy farms. The major agricultural products in Australia, in order of value, are cattle, wheat, dairy, vegetables, fruit, nuts, and lamb meat and wool.

carrots

Map-a-Stat

Australia has more than 134,000 farms that cover around ⅔ of the continent.

There is a measure in South Australia called Goyder's Line, which marks the end of land suitable for crop growing. Land south of the line gets more than

12 inches (30 cm) of rain each year, while land north of the line does not.

Only about 1 percent of Australia's farms use irrigation to water crops.

Each Australian farmer produces enough food to feed 600 people.

The Yarra Valley, in Victoria, is well suited for growing grapes and producing wine.

DO THE MATH!

Use the information in red in the Map-a-Stat box to figure out the following challenge. If each Australian farmer feeds 600 people, and only 150 of those people live in Australia, how many people is each farmer feeding outside Australia? Here is the equation to help you solve the problem.

$$600 \text{ people} - 150 \text{ people} = ? \text{ people}$$

Complete the math challenge, then turn to pages 28—29 to see if your calculation is correct!

Eastern Temperate Forests

Australia has about 482,630 square miles (1,250,000 sq km) of forests. Most of these are **native forests**, but a small number of them are **plantations** where the wood is used for **lumber** and other wood products.

Eucalyptus Trees

When you think about Australia's forests, you probably picture eucalyptus trees. They are home to one of Australia's most famous animals, the koala. Eucalyptus trees make up much of Australia's forests and are **adapted** to the dry climate of the country. They are also adapted to regrow after fires, which are very common on the continent. People use the lumber, oils, and honey made by bees that visit the trees. Aborigines also make many products, including dishes, musical instruments, and canoes, using the wood from the trees.

Orange-thighed tree frogs live in some of the native forests in Queensland.

Map-a-Stat

75 percent of Australia's forests are made up of eucalyptus trees. Much of the remaining forests have acacia and melaleuca trees.

There are around 800 different species of eucalyptus in Australia's forests.

Australia's forests are broken into 8 national forest types, based on the kind of tree that is most prominent.

Rain forests make up 3 percent of Australia's total forested areas.

There are 2,212 species of animals classified as **vertebrates** and 16,836 **nonvascular** plant species in the forests of Australia.

koala

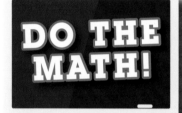

DO THE MATH!

Use the information in red in the Map-a-Stat box to figure out the following challenge. How many times more species of nonvascular plants are there than vertebrate animals living in the forests of Australia? You will need to round your answer. Here is the equation to help you solve the problem.

16,836 plants ÷ 2,212 animals = ? times more plant species

Complete the math challenge, then turn to pages 28—29 to see if your calculation is correct!

temperate rain forest, Victoria

Australia's Rivers

There are 208 major rivers in Western Australia. The largest and best-known river system is the Murray-Darling River Basin. This system is made up of two main rivers and many **tributaries**. The land surrounding these rivers makes up two-thirds of the continent's irrigated farmland.

Sugarcane farms in Australia are often found near rivers.

Lake Cave is a beautiful underground lake in Western Australia.

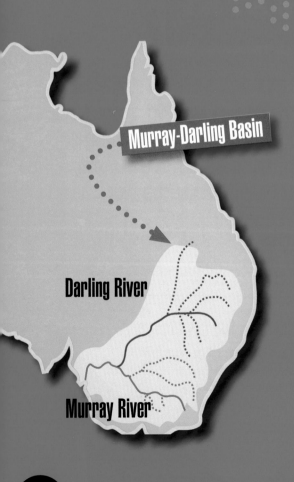

Murray-Darling Basin

Darling River

Murray River

A Unique River

The Gascoyne River is 518 miles (834 km) long. It is unique because for two-thirds of the year, you cannot see it! It is what Australians call an "upside down" river, which means for much of the year this river flows under the ground. It flows above ground for only about 120 days each year.

Map-a-Stat

Australia's longest river is the Murray River, which is 1,558 miles (2,507 km) long.

The second-longest is the Darling River at 960 miles (1,545 km).

The Murray-Darling Basin contains around 30,000 **wetlands**.

At its widest point, the Murray-Darling Basin is 777 miles (1,250 km) across and 848 miles (1,364 km) from north to south.

mouth of the Hopkins River, Victoria

Melbourne, the capital of Victoria, sits on the Yarra River.

DO THE MATH!

Use the information in red in the Map-a-Stat box to figure out the following challenge. If you paddled down the Murray River at a rate of 3 miles per hour, roughly how long would it take you to reach the mouth of the river? You will need to round your answer. Here is the equation to help you solve the problem.

1,558 miles ÷ 3 miles per hour = ? hours

Complete the math challenge, then turn to pages 28—29 to see if your calculation is correct!

Australia's States and Territories

Australia has 6 states and 10 territories. The states are New South Wales, Queensland, South Australia, Tasmania, Victoria, and Western Australia. Each state has its own **constitution** and government. Canberra, the country's national capital, is part of the Australian Capital Territory. Jervis Bay Territory and the Northern Territory are the other territories on the mainland.

This aboriginal rock art shows a fish painted in Kakadu Park in the Northern Territory.

Northern Territory

Queensland

Western Australia

South Australia

Jervis Bay Territory

New South Wales

Australian Capital Territory

Victoria

Tasmania

Big and Small

New South Wales is the state with the largest number of people living in it, while Tasmania has the fewest. The state of Western Australia has the largest area. It is 976,790 square miles (2,529,886 sq km). Few people live there, though. Of its 2.5 million people, most of them live in the southwest corner, near the coast.

Map-a-Stat

New South Wales is the most populated state with a population of 7.5 million people. Tasmania has the smallest population of the 6 states, at 514,700.

It is 745 miles (1,198 km) by road from Brisbane, the capital of Queensland, to Canberra. From Canberra to Melbourne is another 413 miles (665 km).

Central Australian bush country

Queensland is known for its coastal living and surfing.

This is the Sydney Opera House in Sydney, the capital of New South Wales.

DO THE MATH!

Use the information in red in the Map-a-Stat box to figure out the following challenge. By road, how many miles is it from Brisbane to Melbourne, via Canberra? Here is the equation to help you solve the problem.

$$745 \text{ miles} + 413 \text{ miles} = ? \text{ miles}$$

Complete the math challenge, then turn to pages 28—29 to see if your calculation is correct!

Tasmania

Tasmania is 150 miles (241 km) south of Australia. It is the smallest state by area and has the smallest population of any state, too. It is known as the "natural state" because it has so much unspoiled wilderness. In fact, much of Tasmania's land is **protected**, which means it cannot be developed or changed. There are 19 pieces of land that are **reserved** as national parks.

Tasmanian Industry

Tasmania's main industries are mining (especially copper, zinc, tin, and iron), agriculture, forestry, and tourism. Because there is such a large area of wilderness to explore, many tourists come to enjoy the natural beauty of Tasmania. The state has many hotels, two casinos, and several events that draw visitors, as well.

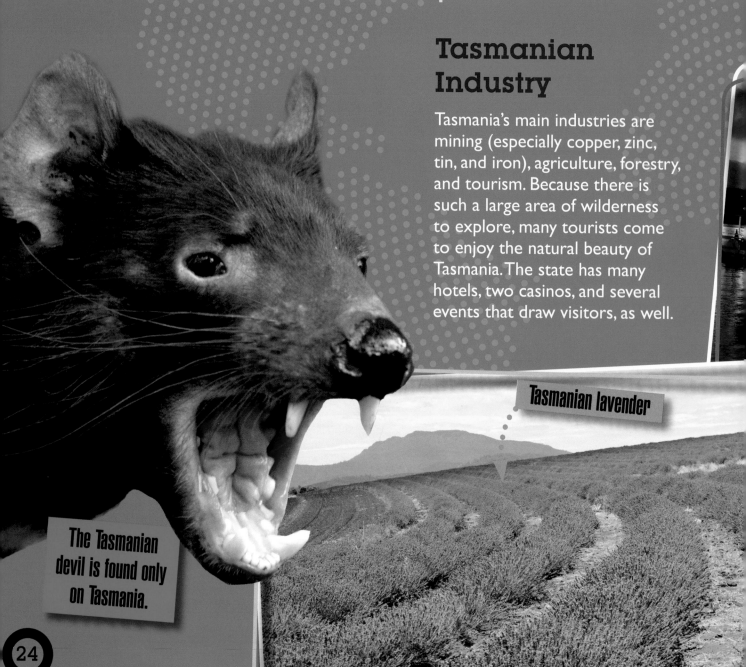

Tasmanian lavender

The Tasmanian devil is found only on Tasmania.

Map-a-Stat

Tasmania's highest point is Mt. Ossa, which stands 5,305 feet (1,617 m) high.

The Tarkine in Tasmania is Australia's largest temperate rain forest. It covers 1,429 square miles (3,700 sq km).

The Tarkine gets up to 94 inches (240 cm) of rain a year. In the Pacific United States, the temperate rain forests there tend to get around 120 inches (305 cm) per year.

900

mainland Australia

Tasmania

Hobart is the biggest city in Tasmania.

DO THE MATH!

Use the information in red in the Map-a-Stat box to figure out the following challenge. How many more inches of rainfall do US temperate rain forests get than the Tarkine? Here is the equation to help you solve the problem.

120 inches – 94 inches = ? inches

Complete the math challenge, then turn to pages 28—29 to see if your calculation is correct!

A Land of Extremes

Australia is a land of **extremes**. It is the smallest and lowest continent. It is the driest inhabited continent, as well. Australia is also famous for its dangerous animals. The saltwater crocodile makes its home in Australia and, at an average of 17 feet (5 m), is the largest crocodile in the world.

saltwater crocodile

Tathra, New South Wales, offers a beautiful sunrise.

The Land Down Under

Australia has huge cattle farms, and grows many vegetables, too. It has **modern** cities and vast areas of unsettled outback. It is a beautiful place and its wilderness areas bring people from other continents, who want to see "The Land Down Under" for themselves.

Map-a-Stat

These beach houses are landmarks of Brighton Beach in Melbourne.

Australia is one of the world's leading **exporters** of coal. It exports more than 332 million tons (301 million mt)! Australia also has some diamond mines.

While English is the main language spoken in Australia, more than 200 languages are spoken there, including 50 aboriginal languages.

Australia's lowest point is Lake Eyre at 49 feet (15 m) below sea level.

Around 85 percent of Australia's population lives within 31 miles (50 km) of the coast.

The world's largest cattle station is in South Australia. It is 9,142 square miles (23,677 sq km), which is larger than New Jersey!

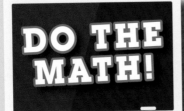

DO THE MATH!

aborigine

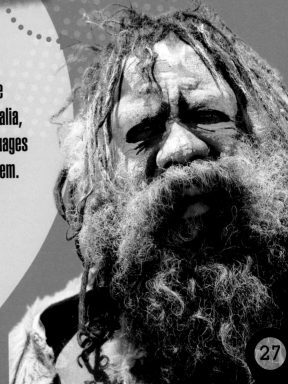

Use the information in red in the Map-a-Stat box to figure out the following challenge. If 50 aboriginal languages are spoken in Australia, and 200 languages are spoken in all, how many non-aboriginal languages are spoken there? Here is the equation to help you solve the problem.

200 languages – 50 languages = ? languages

Complete the math challenge, then turn to pages 28—29 to see if your calculation is correct!

Math Challenge Answers

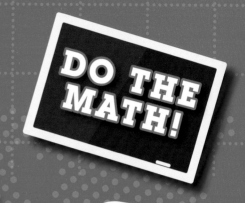

DO THE MATH!

You have made it through the math exploration! How did your math skills measure up? Check your answers below.

Page 5

606 feet + 606 feet
+ 394 feet + 394 feet = 2,000 feet

Page 7

5 + 3 + 1 + 6 + 1
= 16 states and territories

Page 9

22,826 miles ÷ 2 miles per hour = 11,413 hours

Page 11

(1,250 miles × 1 mile per hour) × 2
= 2,500 hours

Page 13

29,035 feet ÷ 7,310 feet
= about 4 times taller

Australia

Glossary

aboriginal Relating to first people to live in Australia.

adapted Changed in order to survive.

amphibian A cold-blooded animal that spends part of its life in water and part on land.

constitution The basic rules by which a country or a state is governed.

continent One of Earth's seven large landmasses.

coral reef An underwater ridge of coral, which is made from the remains of tiny sea creatures. Coral reefs provide a rich habitat for plants and animals.

dingoes Wild dogs that live in Australia.

elevation The height above sea level of an object or area.

exotic Unusual, not often seen.

exporters Countries or people that sell goods to other countries.

extinct No longer existing.

extremes Going past the expected or common. Extreme weather might be very hot or very cold.

fertile Describes ground that is rich and able to produce crops and other plants.

geography The study of Earth's weather, land, countries, people, and businesses.

grasslands Large areas of land covered by grass.

habitats The surroundings where animals or plants naturally live.

irrigation A system of watering farmland.

lumber Wood from trees that have been cut down.

mammals Animals that have warm blood and often fur. Most mammals give birth to live young and feed their babies with milk from their bodies.

modern Using the most up-to-date ideas or ways of doing things.

native forests Forests made up of trees that come from an area or country, rather than those brought into an area or country.

nonvascular Not having a vascular system, which is a series of veins that transport fluid around the body.

plains Large, flat areas of land often covered in grasses.

plantations Large areas on which forests are grown for products, such as rubber and lumber.

plateaus Large, flat areas that are at higher altitude than the surrounding regions.

protected Kept from harm.

reptiles Animals that have scales covering their bodies and that use the sun to control their body temperature.

reserved Set aside as a protected habitat for wildlife.

species A single kind of living thing. All people are one species.

temperate climate Weather that is not too hot or too cold.

territories Particular areas of land that belong to and are controlled by a country.

tributaries Rivers or streams that flow into larger rivers.

vertebrates Animals that have a spine, or a backbone.

wetlands Low-lying areas, such as marshes or swamps, where the ground is saturated with water.

Further Reading

Books

Colson, Mary. *Australia* (Countries Around the World). Chicago, IL: Heinemann, 2012.

Friedman, Mel. *Australia and Oceania* (True Books). Danbury, CT: Children's Press, 2009.

Hirsch, Rebecca. *Australia* (Rookie Read-About Geography). New York, NY: Scholastic, 2012.

Lonely Planet. *Australia: Everything You Ever Wanted to Know* (Not For Parents). Oakland, CA: Lonely Planet, 2013.

Sexton, Colleen. *Australia* (Blastoff! Readers: Exploring Countries). Minneapolis, MN: Bellweather Media, 2010.

Websites

Due to the changing nature of Internet links, PowerKids Press has developed an online list of websites related to the subject of this book. This site is updated regularly. Please use this link to access the list: **www.powerkidslinks.com/me/aust**

Index